MULBERRIES IN RYE

SARAH MORRISH

1

CONTENTS

INTRODUCTION

03/01/17:

You would never call.

You would never call and you would never return a favour – I cannot describe the countless evenings I spent sprawled on the floor, my hair tangled amid the mottled blue carpet, limpid legs cramping in the stillness, the stars penetrating the senses like intergalactic pins and needles. I waited and waited. The phone lit up: *50% Off Pizzas When You Spend £25 Or More!* Unmissable deal. More solitude and silence, though this time paper-weighted with a stomach chock-full of tangy globs and marinara sauce.

I woke up where I fell asleep, mouth rimmed with a mixed herb blend and breath that emanated the funkiest garlic stench known to man (Abraham Van Helsing could only *dream*). You still didn't call and your phone went straight to voicemail, as good as dead. It was then that I realised that you didn't owe me anything but that, in the same vein, I did not owe you anything either; I should stop chasing those who are unwilling to reciprocate the time and respect I put into cultivating and nurturing any given relationship. Take a hint, girl. And then, as though some spirit with an actual *backbone* had inhabited my body, it dawned on me that it is completely okay to outgrow those who had the chance to grow with you but chose to grow apart from you. Sometimes that's a natural curveball, an inevitable towpath the universe will drag you down, but sometimes that person is just not that into you. It happens.

16/10/18:

3

"Would it be ruined if you started taking medication?"

"Would what be ruined?"

"Your creative talent." He raised a tentative eyebrow. I, meanwhile, bathed in the uncomfortable white noise: excuses and explanations lapped at my lips, forget-me-nots glugged around my gullet. Because I wanted the pain to subside but, at the same time, I wanted to succeed even more. It was paramount that I live to verbalise those internal musings, those ripe mulberries congested with bittersweet sap that wanted nothing more than to escape out the ballpoint and spill.

"Perhaps, I guess." Literature: it is my marrow, my bread-and-butter. Call me ignorant, but I never see much (tasteful) material that delves into mental conditions beyond anxiety and depression. Or, I don't know, maybe I'm just not searching hard enough. Because eighteen tiresome years had plodded on before I reached a point in which I felt secure enough to reach out, before a miniscule twinge galled at me and made me realise that it was okay to seek professional help. It did not make me weak and it did not make me more or less valid than anyone else. Over two years have passed and all I have been told is that I "have a mood disorder and an eating disorder" (there are implications, sure, but the prognosis is cryptic at best) but that "it's not depression or anxiety" (another cobbled together 'diagnosis' from a separate doctor).

See, depression and anxiety are horrendous to have to experience and, since both are rather common, deserve to be discussed a ton in mainstream discourse. Their copious coverage means that these struggles have become far more normalised; this is a double-edged sword as whilst these conditions require much support and fellowship, it also means they tend to be reduced to frivolous adjectives, words emblazoned on budget merchandise, at the expense of those who have to live with it. But, on the whole, it is great that more people are starting to feel a little more comfortable in verbalising their mental illnesses and — fingers crossed! — receiving adequate help. I must admit, though, that I continue to battle with the fact that my ambiguous condition will continue to stigmatise me, even demonise me, and continue to read as atypical to write on with such freedom. And, let me stress, this is not to suggest that one given condition

4

is 'worse' or 'harder' than another; I just live as though I am in limbo, as though the entire universe is a sodden minefield that I am preparing to lob a thousand blind grenades towards. In short: I still feel underrepresented. I still feel like an anomaly.

24/03/19:

One poem per evening. I write best when its night-time, when the stars remove their hats and the universe is static. Pounding on idle keys, a rosebud sipping — no! gulping! — on rosé; this is, perhaps, the twenty-first century equivalent to an aristocratic scholar standing atop a cliff cursing at the wind, yelling his woes into the ether in the eighteen-hundreds.

But, to be honest, it's not even about writing 'best.' I don't write to impress other people, to flex those literary muscles. I don't even write to be read! And, though I hope you appreciate this collection and that it allows you to experience *something*, I tend not to think upon the way a statement might be construed as I'm creating it. Decent art should have no universal concord — it should not be manufactured with one desired emotional response in mind, one sole interpretation. That is because, as individuals, we do not emote the same, we do not theorise and speculate the same, we do not live under the same conditions or circumstances. That we are not raised as uniform humans should mould the manner in which we perceive a text; an acquaintance of mine believes that Vincent Van Gogh's *Starry Night* comments upon religion, whilst I believe it's just an aesthetic landscape. There is no right or wrong. Because art that requires an explanation is not good art, is not purposeful art. Have you ever been stuck in a room whilst some overbearing, overenthusiastic pick-me tells a joke and it just lingers in the air so, after deciding that a five-second pause implies his audience doesn't understand, goes on to run them through what makes it amusing? It's that.

And, in a similar vein, writing can be cathartic so long as I'm not overthinking it, hence the sporadic punctuation, the odd metre, the inconsistent form, the shit blind line drawings. It is not polished, or

5

methodical, or esteemed, or even *that* presentable. The actual content can yo-yo between the ambiguous, the sombre, and the rousing. Let it be made clear that this is not a self-help guide! It goes without saying but, when I write about super disturbing moments, I'm not seeking to promote or romanticise the toxic thoughts or the destructive behaviours that accompany them. And on that note, some sections (read: the first section) need a big ol' trigger warning stamped on them because the material is sensitive: we're talking alcoholism, substance abuse, death, eating disorders, depression, panic attacks, self-harm. And, as I mentioned, it might be disturbing but that's almost the point; it's unfiltered and autonomous because life *can be* disturbing sometimes - why sugar-coat it? But I hope the second and third sections allow you to appreciate that it doesn't always have to be that way. There is a light.

RAW RYE

Section One

storm in a teacup

i wish i had been prepared

to weather the rain, the

minor inconveniences and

the inconsequential blights

that are not *supposed* to

ache but maim like bleach

in a six-inch gouge.

impossible

hammer and chisel — they are concrete
jungle dreams. hallucinations interlaced
with high-street heroin and homemade
tourniquets. cheap chip wrappers and
bearded men in rags and open-topped
sandals who beg and launder and pester
and mug. there is graffiti on the stained
cream wall: *free the people*. no one cares
but to paint over their war-cries and
hope they melt away.

getting bad again

another ripped petal cascades to the concrete
where the earth lends no shelter. it is harsh
and exclusive. it does not heed newcomers.
one petal drops as the wind captures it in a
gargantuan inhale and another petal leaps to
its death with intent and purpose. one petal
sobs as it dangles on a gimcrack thread.
another petal is ripped clean from the carpel
and stomped on. trodden underfoot. the flower
is naked again. her identity and inclination
violated. she stands alone. without those petals
she is powerless and destined to weep in the
autumn.

to know him is to miss him

you are a maypole adorned

in rainbow sheen, doted on

with the rolling of the sun

and the turning of the moon.

straining to harmonise until

each abuts their tune: a

silver flute. i dont want to

have to miss you. the notes

cut into my conch and make

it bleed. it is far too soon.

baby

i should not have to

spoon-feed you into

treating me as an

equal.

a shift in perception

the first time i lit a cigarette i

was thirteen and did not have a

match or a lighter at my disposal,

so i shoved the end into the

red-hot toaster and ran into the yard.

no cough or splutter did transpire,

but nothing tethered me to nicotine

either — no impulse did shadow

me thither. i coddled that cigarette

at thirteen cause i wanted to

live; now i inhale because i do not.

gulliver

hourglass turned on its head
inverted and nanoscopic. he
whittled as a grain: lilliputian
pieces venturing to another
realm. to the other side. and
she could do little but watch.
netted curtains and stained
glass muddle.

bad intentions

your words hurt more than

your blades or your

bullets.

the morning after the night before

the morning after the night before

i recalled the pigment that danced

upon the moleskin notebook with

terrifically assured vigilance and

vigour. the forcing of the pen, like

the forcing of the hand, serves to

remind me that everything

is not okay.

the morning after the night before

i could not help but decipher

the scrawls scribbled upon my skin

as the master dagger brimmed

with determination, denial, and purpose

and told me, tipsy as a treasure map,

that i had struggled and it hurt.

calorie

sustenance coalesces with

serotonin so that it melds

a menace: a spurious hijacker

who has thwarted the controls

and assumed captaincy.

and now i am on autopilot.

we are one.

internalised

i recognise your footsteps as they pound on up the stairs before i unearth the hardships those feet had to run from. i catch those eyes across the dinner-table as we chumble and chomp down on our food without contemplating what prior trepidations those eyes may have had to witness. i listen to a voice that is connected to a brain that is desperate to barter with the body i spy across the room. it is a pedantic brain that fusses and fawns and pricks and prods until the footsteps quieten down and the eyes glaze over and the voice starts to tremble with each solemn syllable. and i wonder what on earth you are worried about until i realise that we are one and the same.

broken record

together we are a turntable

she the vinyl and i the needle

she the blighted groundhog

and i the stuttering invigorator

that she discusses over martinis

with her new loves instead.

routine

i know what happens when you bolt
the bathroom door shut and cuss at
the world and its pollution. i know
the rusted blade is a charmer but he
is cold and will not bring you solace.
i have met the keloid molehills that will
burrow across your arm; they ache in
their surliness and are not welcome in
this house anymore.

hurt

its been three-hundred-and-nine hours

and that is time enough. faces turn

into heads as woollen façades begin

to unravel all slow and cathartic:

he was not that special.

shovel down that last glob of cookie

dough. vacuum that rosé up.

remember that he would still

be around if he was.

youre all cried out; youre hoover

dam in drought season nibbling

on saltine crackers and stirring up

dustbowls with your scuffed old

trainers that have been but two-hours

reacquainted with the fresh air

and the rude paving slabs where the
dandelions violate the crevices.

but a guttural guffaw pierces the
trombones thumping at your throat.
there he goes! swivel on your heels
as his glide over the cobbles whilst
a nymph paws at his arm,
garlands in her hair and giddiness
on the wind's current. and it hurts
not because she is interchangeable
with you, but because he lied.

innumerable im-not-readys and
im-not-looking-to-move-on-yets.
you have heard it so many times
from so many dull and uninspiring

men with no backbone and no
other word combinations sloshing
around up there. and it will
always be a fucking lie and it
will *always* feel like a broomstick
through the eye socket.

isnt pain supposed to hurt less
and less, the more accustomed
you become to the sensation? isnt
that what the old wives say?
untrue. he is not a papercut
or a thorn in your side,
he is a cancer.

snort

the grindstone doth proclaim that it is law

thus the avalanche must therefore ensue

and the pastel pulvilio should caw

at the septum that the dust tries to chew.

shovelled into me – a drag and a draw –

a snowstorm one grows to love and accrue.

giving and receiving

i saluted the sun as he fanned at

my face and furnaced my bones.

you never did that. not even

once.

my bedroom is a mess

sounds poetic, no?

i stumble home and disrobe. the dress i wore

is bundled beside the door like a vagrant.

the suede heels that did blister and blunt

are strewn this direction and that.

i cannot think. mind like glaucoma.

still etched in the makeup two men

smudged and one girl ribbed. the water

bottle has befriended the carpet: a limb

must have knocked it as i slept.

what does it mean that my textbooks

lie spread eagle beneath the desk and

gather dense dust? clogged arteries.

it is an ending to an evening and it is

a frustrated exhale but — as with

every single ending — it promises a

chance to start over.

<u>out of office</u>

this pen is deceased

the ink has run out

and the lead in this

pencil has snapped.

this keyboard wont

type and these hands

will not write because

the mind that controls

them has crashed.

bruises and grazes

cartwheels and catherine wheels

they whomp, whomp thud and strike

sartorious or plantaris born to be

clipped. butterfly wings?

it stings! she's fallen and she

can't arise! she cries and,

caterwauling on a concrete

slab, the slab begins to

melt away, amalgamate!

you are quite safe, dear.

wounds dont heal

overnight, but give it time.

bruises brew and bump

and stew, but it subsides

and we all turn blue. grazes

shout; don't hear them out

as they fade and they

fade and they fade into you.

red flags and warning signs

the moment he does something to you

that you would not condone someone

doing to your daughter is the moment

you must leave.

twenty-six hours fasted: two hours sleep

featherweight —

the teeth grind against

one another until they

are blunt and the stomach

starts to wail. it gnaws at

itself from the inside out

like a washing machine

on spin and drain and spin

again, burbling a bloodied

pang laced with dopamine

and cocaine.

lobotomy for one

seven paces transverse. nine paces steep.

there is no shallow water here.

no company to keep.

i was born into this chamber!

i dream it when i sleep.

condemned to sink beneath its soil;

indivisible and deep.

panic attack

taut as a bolt — porcelain sclera

pried open. ventriloquists mistress

hoisted up uncut on matchsticks

and metallic grooves that howl at

a lacerated waterline. palpitations!

ephemeral failure and flatline enmeshed

into one silent scream that the mouth

scrambles to mime. a nadsat collywobble.

alas! no ear can receive it and it makes no

ends 'cause would it even matter if they

could?

swallow

she gnaws on eiderdown

peonies. swirls them

around her mouth and gulps

until the blood runs

crimson and the

sandpaper screams.

the other woman

i cannot escape you

even in dreaming.

dormant and benumbed,

i watch you swaddled in white

linen that creases as you stir,

cappuccino soaking your

breath after breakfast

as you pull her closer

and push me farther

into hopelessness.

it's a disease

the streetlamps were screaming as you
meandered into the road with a head
filled with a genocide and a hand
clutching whiskey in rye. your knuckles
were reddened — windsnapper — bullfighter —
and your breath smelled like overdue
rent. you muttered about nothing at all
until nothing dressed up as everything
and it all spurted out as the rain beat down:
that you did not care if you were dead in
ten years and that existence was one big
sham. the next day it was more of the same
with a drip in your arm and a mistruth itching
to cross your lips.

more than an upset

hot cross buns. i would rip the raisins out and
save them. trimmed grass. the chamomiles
would excrete pollen and entice the bees into
a stupor. intoxicated on nature. his armchair.
deserted and marooned. a pillow and a
crochet throw assembled like a cultivated ruin
or a sepia photograph. he was seldom there.
an imprint in a home that started to turn into
a house. a hospital bag on the stairwell. i
would paint him a picture once in a while so
that i could be with him in pigment. so that
his clinical space might become vibrant and
vivacious. like he was. the crayons were
mottled where these nimble adolescent hands
could not put on pressure but the men and
women were rapturous and the rolling hills

were ample. not a cross cloud sat overhead.
each blade and each thistle harmonised. cheap
notepad paper peeled and torn. he plastered
them on the walls. lined them. i have not
seen them since. i have not seen him either.

giovanna says

"starve the tissue that entombs me

so that the bones might obtrude

and this chest might flatten and

these hips be less wide than they

are. the universe expects so

much from a frame that i

hate with anatomy i hate in a

society that i hate and who hates

me in return."

obsolete #9

my soul is numb and a spirit cannot dull

the sheer pain, the immense longing

for wanting to be gone. god, i wish i

were gone and blessed with no life

at all for i would wither into the

shadows and become a mere

tree or a piece of bracken or heather

on a hillside by a carn. gentle, and

sensual and unbothered and alone.

black holes in the sky

she told me that my eyes looked so very empty — i told her that i cannot remember what it means to be full.

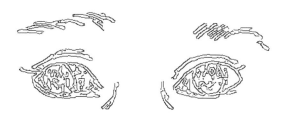

bulimic knuckles

i am bruised and reddened and wretched

from retching! retching till the bile runs clear;

till vomit paints the vacuous visage

that birthed it into the nearest cup or

bag or plughole; till the heart cavorts and

the stomach rips clean down the middle, a

sandbag obscene and unco terminal.

i am void. vision totters into an

analogue migraine and the brain that did

promise so very much can deliver so

very little.

a pondering on casual consent

why must it take an *i-have-a-boyfriend*

to get you to leave us alone? i find it

most peculiar that a woman can decline

an advance and will continue to be harassed

until it is implied that she is with another man.

is that because a man and his relationship

is more sacred to you than the relationship

between a woman and her own autonomy –

her own decision-making and ability to

choose?

how many pictures of wizened genitalia should

a woman have to endure? how many pick-up

lines steeped in violent innuendo? how many

adjectives – *prude* or *whore* or *bitch* – shall

be tossed around because she refuses to be

your glory hole?

loose ends: unemotional

dead-end —

no through

road.

drained —

barren. devoid.

tearless.

there is

nothing that

remains.

<u>types</u>

i see me in you

and i see her in me

and that must be

frightening for you.

x marks the spot

let us observe

the sparrow-breathed

stillness in the

tumbledown shed as

an all-british

gigolo with a curvature

in his spine and

a dagger in his hand

plunges the prong

into her shoulder

blade with

precision and

ambition --

a regular ibn

battuta itching

to unearth the

blotch that

begs to be

perforated until

it weeps red

plush.

feed me

there is something for

everyone but nothing

for me. i am starving

and putrid and lonesome.

a note on the bosnian genocide: in memoriam

bloodshed overspills into teacups where

the potsherds invade the grašak and it tastes

like petrification: an eradication and a silence.

an erasure that extends beyond the supposed

cleanse that the brutes tried to implement but

to the point where the crime as an historical

event and its details came to be denied. there

is no reason to protect such ruthlessness and

insist that women and children were spared.

that is much besides the point. no one

deserves to sidle around with dartboards fixed

to their foreheads. we will remember the fallen.

my medication

a decade without resolution or rime:

fine! seize the controls! i am all

vodka and rum with insides

blackened and tarred and

pills that hook themselves

to the walls that i bash this

porcelain brain into when it

has bleated its morning prayers.

i cannot even muster a tear.

evacuee

why do i continue to

evacuate myself?

now all my tomorrows

are gone

desecration

harvest moons have passed and

yet a jealous pang continues to

molest me whenever you carry

her name on your lips as though

she is as weightless as oxygen

and i am as heavy as an anvil.

used

notice how he will atone when he
knows that your legs are spread.
sorry bore no substance two hours
prior. he didnt need to apologise;
you pushed him too hard and he
snapped. disinterested. dismissive.
but now you are his platter. his
sustenance. an all-you-can-eat.
he would opt for six heaped plates.
paper plates. as disposable and
worthless as his insincere pardon.

changeling

we sat beneath an elm. our spines shared

secrets with the lichenous bark. tittering

betwixt themselves. jeering at the peonies.

we draw mugs to our mouths. saucerless.

the steam infiltrates our nostrils and fogs

up our glasses. "does it taste different

to you?" "yes. it does."

cuts

much like a live wire

a fuse destined to

short-circuit

it burrows deeper and

crawls underneath

strewing cauterised

vermillion brickwork

in its wake

"im so proud of you"

those words tickle at my throat −

razor slashes. glitched patchwork

that i cannot compute because i

do not deserve the sentiment,

cannot knit together the syllables

on a spool that will smash and

a yarn that will rip. i am no

martyr; i am dented.

the master surgeon

i am botched: i have always been botched
and not because a magazine or social media
told me so. i want to grab scissors and cut
the fat from my body so that i am clean
bone. i want to take a scalpel to my face and
rearrange every little thing i hate. tell me im
sane. tell me im happy. i dont care whether
you think im pretty.

reflections

i had always been told

that the eyes are the

mirrors to the soul. but

let it be made known

that mirrors distort

our images: widen and

reverse them. our

dysmorphia trembles

at gunpoint.

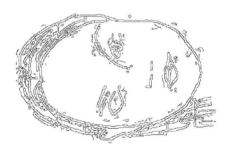

what i mean to state is

that i have never peered

into my own soul. never
can and never will be able
to see my eyes through
someone elses. a camera
cannot replicate the
sensation, the aura. i wonder
what i haemorrhage: is it
pride or is it pain?

i dine on your heart

the maggot is spellbound

within and without an

apple, deep bottle green

and bruised to the touch.

it burrows within its atrium

as i bite into its ventricle

crisp and manic, an endless

river bloodstained a

bellicose red.

i abstain

a hole in the heart! a bullet

in the rib! i isolate and deprive

so that another hand may never

touch this flesh or violate this brain

with deception and lore. i will not

let it happen again. you ruined me.

strength and earning

do not stand aside and present us with space.
that is too simple. we are not your good
deeds or your tokenistic trophies. we have
muscled into spheres deemed untouchable and
unattainable our entire lives. what makes you
think we will stoop now?

MULBERRIES IN RYE

Section Two

evolution

i am tired of answering to men

who have serpentine lips and opal hearts,

multicoloured loincloths and vizards.

glass goblets congested with statements –

promises that are never upkept –

are hoisted atop their cloud-covered heads.

"glove your hand, lads! and glove your heart,"

the unspoken doctrine revealed.

there was a young man who lived in a

pinecone, placed on parisian cobbles

where the streets smell like rye and cigars.

he is worn and weathered, with a soul

made unable to love anymore.

and it is this that he told me

that november night, though not in

so many words. *v* with which the word

vain begins drawls all around my matter.

but why must i cling to a pinecone

when a chestnut rests on the tuscan streets?

pour qui veut chasser, one muses,

and leaves the trick-sparrow behind.

let me stress: i am in no hurry

to understand what i mean or do not,

or who i may be or have yet to

be. i am young, there is time, and i know

this pinecone will untangle his

prongs, and a chestnut he will become.

mixed messages

you water me and

then you weed me

out and i cannot

decide whether to

weep or to wilt,

to bloom or to bud.

inbreathe

i yearn to breathe you into my lungs,

in through the nose and out through the

mouth. it is a deliberate inhale,

long and intense, and saturates each

bronchus and lobe with pertinent punch.

i want to lull in your chimney smoke,

as you swamp through the air and mar it

with your wooden scented shining splints –

punctured carina aglow.

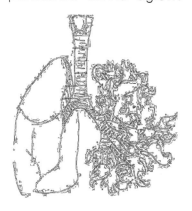

incompatible

how can i feel complete

when my body did not

allow you to enter me?

it took a second attempt.

i was a crippled machine

that could not compute

why a rectangle could not

coalesce with a square.

we were meant to be one.

you and me

he is tattooed

onto my brain,

encoded into

my flesh.

i am an impotent

anecdote, an

unattached number

in an ancient

phone.

this is a sign to shoot your shot

cupid! merciless mercantile,

inadequate archer. sharpen

up the utensil: master the bow

and dominate the arrow.

whiplash.

misfires meld contingencies,

construct closure, and resolve

the vacillation that pesters

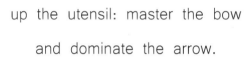

in the night. and one day

that dart will pierce the

right heart and you shall

be glad that you shot.

the gardener

i ache because i wonder how it

must feel to be touched and tended

by a hand who will nourish your

bulbs and your blooms and nurture

your weeds and wildflowers

one crepuscolo at a time

the tiber frames the roman soil

with laps of scintillating teal

that peak and trough and glint in the

glare where the sun declares war

on the pilgrims' foreheads – come one,

come all! – as their wearied feet plod

to saint peter's throne, eternal

and heralded acute. time doth

chisel at his cheek and set in

as gault might; his neolithic

ruins are born to be breached.

and that was supposed to be me.

die liebe des plato

foxtrot, sheepskin, crocodile

tears that flagellate each

girlchild and her girlfriend.

metal canes smack. leather

shackles and spurs submerged

in complete shadow. flogged

chaps. cat o' nine — is that the

time? — lash at mannequins in sordid

boudoirs where no one cares to

learn your name. little plastic

woman, a sweetie, a puppy-dog

on a studded leash: ball-and-chain.

drown me in that bathtub (i wont

tell). scream! venus sheds her

furs stooped on a pompous knee.

she with a pompadour. backcombed

beehive militia — they bite! — stand clouded in a dungeon where the air smells like sex and candy and looks just like heroin. she will pluck the stems from her strawberries and feed you to the worms. call it love.

dearly beloved

panpipe dream with effervescent green

cradled around thy clandestine shape.

treacle mirage as delicate as

a cotton-candied carousel ride

with scorched embers rattling within.

beloved was he, pentecostal

dream, reduced and transformed into soil,

anonymous dust skirting the shore −

an old man's memory, a sallow

epitaph pledged unto a crumbling stone.

feminism

the moment that your feminist parosuel

refuses to sheath older women,

trans women, queer women,

larger women, immigrant women,

women of colour, poorer women,

incarcerated women, abused women,

women are not as abled, is the

moment that your feminism

stands as still as a sun-dial

in a thunderstorm. you are

not a feminist.

exultation

there was a time in which we ran
as parallel lines beneath the sand
but the tide has since erased
the evidence we made and now
you live with denial tattooed plain
on your brain. the tide moves in
me as you did too and suffice to
say each gasp we drew screamed
exultation and confusion.

the 'it' debacle

is he worth it?

how am i supposed to know

when im forward-facing

double-dutching through

a marbled mosaic and

im not sure what 'it' is?

for a blue boy

your eyes are like oceans —

i get lost in them. i kick and i

scream and wade up to my

waist where the tide overlaps

and the azure pool breaks into

froth that's like coffee crema. it

carries me on its compliant current

straight into the whirlpool.

attachment and experience

he is not the same as them.

we are not all cut from the

same cloth and you know that

to be true. each person is a

lesson. please dont wave a

pendulous thunderbolt over

his head because someone

else treated you with

malcontent and

thoughtlessness.

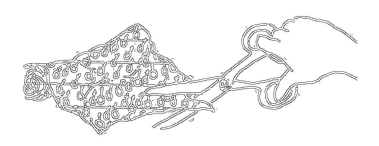

open up

it is not courageous to man a
makeshift dam that is liable to
gush out its contents at once.

pillbox hat

but it wears you! the sublime

organdie wisps about that double-crown. it

is status and it is class, darling.

shade: caricature in pastiche. how

opaque must that head feel now?

nail varnish atop a red balloon.

listless and dense yet oh-so-opulent.

in case you were confused:

just because the honey pot is

sticky does not mean that the

dipper was invited in.

too much

the universe must

have been

on opium when it

carved that

gilded flesh and

warmed that

peach cobbler heart.

i love to

see you naked.

tesoro's inferno

you are a fire

a raging, unapologetic fire

and i wish — sometimes —

i could be just like you

but you wont take no

for an answer

yet no means no.

theres a difference between

a kindling in your belly and a

combustion in your soul

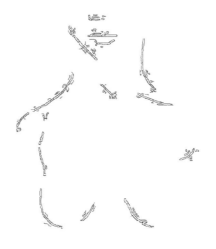

chameleon

who do you think you are? leonard

cohen or some temperamental

troubadour? a sexed-up dolly or

a righteous little sibyl? an intoxicated

ego or a cataclysmic id? you

are everything are nothing

at the same time.

<u>Y O U</u>

as tender as the

waves that roll

around my ankles

and caress each

grain of sand.

on emotional instability

my mind is a palette. method and madness
and scant titillations. it is blue for the sadness
and purple for the bruises; scarlet for the lust
and yellow for the glee. it seems each must
make love with one another to generate this
emotional stream – extremes and forgiveness
and hatred and inoculation. and, pray tell,
what would i be without this than a shell?

matchbox

he was his match and he

was his phosphorous

together working in

tangent to create something

marvellous yet flammable.

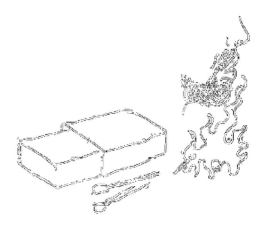

my friend sivvy

hell-flames collapse into concave charcoal

as the spineless spindled woodworm reaps

rings on the cedar dresser. salt in her blood —

pencil-marks. each one collateral and

catastrophic. deviant in disaster:

an open wound liaises with bleach — a

mulberry lesion on unblemished flesh.

excavate the tome where the polaroids

perish; her countenance a dirtied smear.

thats how he liked it. pensive eagle: scalped.

heave and claw at extramarital sin.

his great mouth unhinged clean at the jaw and

devoured her whole. does that make it
poignant? obsess over each word when she
leaves and scout for clues. a shamed obituary:

a nuance; cliché; sullen cloud; someone
to outgrow or be dismissed in discourse.
gaslighted − suppressed − invalidated.

perennial memoirs

somersaults and catherine

wheels. we collide and

collapse into chapters

and chronicles as our

nails scratch at the

pencil-thin papyrus.

i'll be your seashell

i'll be your seashell

melded in coral and magnolia

where the shoreline meets the sea

and the tide piledrives into

those sad craters that your

footprints made so that new

ones shall evince.

i'll be your seashell

that converses with the sunset to

ensure that you will be taken care of

as the sand becomes cold beneath your toes

and the brackish mist turns cruel and ruder.

i'll be your seashell

that roars when you draw me toward your ear

so that you might remember your first nest

and let me sing you into a dream. the

world wasn't ready.

be direct.

stop hoping that people will

notice you are not okay. those

who are worth it will notice

as soon as you turn down that

coffee. as soon as you smile

with no gumption. as soon as

you punctuate your sentences.

to be known is to be understood.

but we are not all mind-readers.

analogue

unbutton the noise!

it is a harsh peacoat,

a tinnitus. it mangles

your head and stomps

on your heart. shrug

off those layers and

breathe.

mulberry in rye

it is hard to accept

that you are little

more than a mulberry

trodden underfoot

juice writhing

amid the meadow

whilst he is rye

your whiskey would not be

the same without it

no gumption no bite no

volitional sabotage

snowchild

those footprints embedded in snow

remind me that i am neither a

gazelle nor an antelope who

is able to trot with decorous

elegance. eat up! a scant little

snowberry whistles at the wind.

catcalls it. the shepherds never

warned me about *this*: nimbostratus

dipped in a salmon bouquet. it

will cover these steps in the morn

and so it will baptise me. resurrection.

cherry-picker red liquor boy

i love you in the sunshine as the

curtains curtail the window and

are punctuated in the warmth

and wind. the air drapes about

that golden halo atop your head

with curls that scale the dense clouds

and kiss the gentle mountaintops

hello as though it were *goodbye*.

it is an embrace that is imprinted

upon an inlet and is eternal and

messianic in its sheer omnipotence.

you were a soothsayer and a

prophet in a whirlwind.

i love you in the monsoon that

hammers on the slate and bedews

the granite beneath us. we nurse

a cast iron stovetop which becomes

our melting pot and orchestrates

the billowing steam whilst our

fingers slog in rhyme and

purr at wooden spoons. i wander

in my time (for we are not

special) but amble past the

shower as you croon to sam cooke;

the waterfall must pour upon

your head as you pour into me

so we might become one again.

let's talk about sex

isnt it peculiar how

those who pride their

sexuality on exploiting

our sexuality come to

hate us when we choose

to be sexual on our own

terms without their say-so.

quench my thirst

you are water

and i am parched.

a fairytale union

once upon a cherubic harpsichord

memories made love on her sleeve.

panpipes quivered as he keeled at

the knees. mise-en-scene like a

siamese dream. each shone within

one another. irreversible in their

compression: golden locks with

misplaced keys.

"wear a bra"

it is so disheartening to hear such words

escape a mouth that has been held hostage

to a domineering patriarchal discourse,

the same one that her mother and her mother

endured. that same oppressive – suppressive –

climate that tells me i am being suggestive

when a nipple nicks at a sweater. who knew

two lard-filled ice-cream scoops designed

to nurse a child could incite such blind

vexation? it disappoints me that you tell me i

should cover up more when the electrician

comes over to fix the meter as though it is

my breasts' responsibility to ensure that he

does not touch or ogle me without permission.

i can wear as much or as little as i like:

i owe him nothing.

lowercase crisis

forget uppercase and forget commas and

colons. who fed you that bait?

the same institutionalised androids who led

you to believe that the british empire

was productive and positive and that

christopher colombus discovered america!

fuck what you heard. world

runs amok: fools

and their mindless

consumption.

there are more ways than one to be rich

cash does not equate sense

or moral status. richness

is brewed deep within. i would

rather be remembered as

someone who could help

a friend than someone who

burnt a bill next to a homeless

person as a dare. i would rather

be remembered as an intelligent

and courageous woman than

someone who owned five houses

whilst most will never own one.

and whilst it is true that one can

spend their own wealth as they

choose that does not mean their

vapid lack of richness in character

does not radiate in the manner

their consciences are so alarmingly

skewed.

sunny-side

this is communion,

cordial and conservative where

the eggs are sunny-side up

and the pan is non-stick.

lecherous batter bubbles

to a cookie cutter strain

and the neon kitchen

commoditised and fetishised

glows under a treacle heat

that sandwiches your

mouth closed like a beartrap

and mauls the senses to shreds.

fixation

you were not a movie star but
rather an egon schiele painting:
anatomical and raw in your
sexual exuberance. you need not
utter a word nor draw a scowl
and the tulips would still
decapitate themselves. theyre
timid in your presence.
blushing petals so coquettish
and bashful. you charm their
strands back together — you
are like glue.

my greatest friend

you imbibe me with livelihood because

you either accentuate or totally numb the

hurt or the mirth, the ache in the sunset

or the solace in the sunrise.

and i feel alive again.

farewell gentlemen

farewell gentlemen.

the cabaret was in town

and the bodacious bunnies

leapt out from their six-tier

desserts; i suppose that you

retired to bed with them

instead. farewell gentlemen.

saxophones abound shrivelled

limes and acerbic lemon zest

cannot disguise the whiskey

in rye on my breath.

a happy accident

a scowl plunged into a nest

atop a ponderosa pine and

somersaulted along an anorexic

avenue where the yarrow stands

to attention swinging its silver

baton at the ladies in gleaming

convertibles. i long for disaster

and i wish to lord over it.

a reflection on a lost cause

what did i see in him?

i bemoan to the girls

over whiskey in rye

and we all roll our eyes

and scoff at the men

who have scorned us before.

i wonder whether i muse on

such trivialities because i have

changed or because i have not

the most authentic charlatan in town

i bathe in fools gold

because i dont know

who i am anymore

and i do not care to

find out.

when the optimism outweighs the pessimism

openness can leave you

vulnerable but openness

can turn a hand into a heart.

why it matters

ruminate on this: the universe came into existence not five billion years ago. heed the banal old trope that claims the older one gets the wiser one gets and imagine! imagine how wise our planet must be and how much wisdom one earth can muster in that span. it is us who championed adam and eve and the void that existed prior to their instalment in the ample garden. and it is us who discuss the dinosaurs with fervour and scrutinise their remains under microscope lenses hoping to glean a landscape prisoner to time. and it is us who idealise ancient egypt and brand it synonymous with the pyramids and cleopatra with complete inattention to the fact that the latter was born closer to the advent of the cell phone than the construction of the former. ones sunset is anothers sunrise. doesnt that put things into perspective? we are little more than

parasitic gnats that are hellbent on sentencing the

planet to death with our sacrilege and our electric

chairs —

oh! to be human is to serve a life sentence: the

average totals seventy-nine years. some we lose too

soon whilst some are born to live. that is but an

appetiser in the banquet we call the planet and its

past. sure, we have coloured television (should one

so much as grace our living room anymore) but our

social progress is ambiguous. it is a lemon pancake

or a pink grapefruit: bittersweet. a mere five-

decades-plus-six-years ago high school students

were compressed against concrete walls. the water

gushed. leviathan humiliation under tyrannical

doctrine. bullish. the most segregated city in the

country so said doctor king. the panthers did prowl but huey did perish. and so have numerous unarmed individuals since — blameless lambs led to institutional torture chambers cemented in the muttons systematic sand lime. the lynch is lauded. belly-up. bones bled bare. and white people cannot call someone the n-word so it all must compensate mustnt it? but the bias continues to exist: oppressor. but the hurt continues to exist: oppressed. because either could have been your (YOUR) grandmother or grandpa out there. and that is the reason the scrimmage still matters because the timeline is insubstantial; these atrocities are crammed into the shallowest graves and the tiniest boxes known to man.

redemption poem

it was when i started crushing mulberries beneath my
feet and watching their juices intermix with the grass
that I realised i could turn wine into water. i had the
power to turn solid into liquid. to cleanse and to
redeem my psyche for i have sinned.

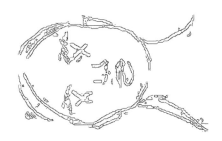

PEART MULBERRIES

Section Three

a choice

i have the choice

to cultivate a forest.

it will sprout from

my flesh and i will

tend it as often

or as little as i

choose. i am

entitled to my woodland

for it is my own,

and it cannot

be scythed.

ode to kusama

a dot is an infinite assertive irradiation that can humble one and can slap one so cool and cumbersome till the opening melts their horizon into candlewax spawning harmonious fountains among lily-pads anew. the artist is a phantasmagoria in an eggshell tempered a marvellous violet and liable to combust into a million small fragments so that she can soar or paddle to her waist in seaweed – cyclical washing machine.

the path is my own

isnt it charming? to shove my fingers

into pies and lick the cream clean off

as they command the paper and coax

the fountain pen that is employed to

forge a fate that is changeable and

malleable and entirely my own

a jeremiad for unrealised potential

old mister smith shines shoes in his shop,

polishes with zeal as the sun plummets

down over the greyscale horizon.

silver threads dance atop his head and sweat

beads moisten his brow that is blemished with

time and a subconscious rue. he mourns that

which could have been but never came to

be; he mutters under his breath so that

no one can hear (since it does not count

when words do not meet with a gallant ear).

he laments in memoriam and weeps

subdued for the cold corona dream

that the sceptical rabble deemed null.

doused in the humdrum

reverie supressed

in an hourglass that

he thought upon.

once.

there's a man cut in two by the window

there's a man cut in two by the window

and his shoes cannot nibble at the ground

his torso hangs skew, slanted and ergo

no friend do his trousers have to be found.

a timepiece, ancient, rests at his elbow

but, embalmed in calm, does not make a

sound because it too must be severed in two

oh!—the maid's wild cries shall surely ensue.

"god! it is him! make haste!" cried the servant.

red is her apron, no one hears her call.

his jigsaw she tries to amend – fervent,

but her master is dead, she starts to bawl.

"where, though, is madam?" she peers east and south,

swings open the door – dead! foam at her mouth.

penna and buccarelli

dama penna rode with buccarelli

into the stained-glass mosaic where the

sunset tasted like emblazoned nectar

and thawed out like venetian candlewax

as the dusk kissed the dawn and said

goodbye. the palominos captured the crescent

on their coats, inscribed in silken ardour;

their hooves sailed across the masegni and

caressed the eiderdown embraces from

lovers who came to pass, perennial

marble men and nymphic gilded ladies.

gondolas bobbed on velvet wavelets that

lapped with the coming, coming and going

and not at all mercurial but hush.

dama penna remained unperturbed and

noble; she purred and roosted just to be

pandered and cared not (oh--! cuore mio!)

that the tide would assault piazza san

marco and bayonet the palazzo

dandolo - non c'è modo! – so long as

her lavenders on the veranda did

not drown. buccarelli was a writer:

she thumbed ancient tomes in crimson

smatters and embraced the men and women

who danced around the tadpole river where

the dawn met the dew - people-watching. she

reclined on hillsides sipping at her merlot and

dining on her tramezzino in a

cradle imbued with gladioli and

geraniums. *mi amore, is it*

true that the lavenders are wilting

under strychnine sunbeams, scared the moon can

rest no more? oh--! muse into the shadow

and ponder. there is so much we can do.

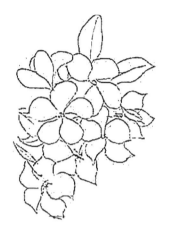

fourteen cream plumerias

romance creeps into these walls —

a white cadillac in pursuit

carbonised like spectres in pompeii.

the doorbell antagonises my slumber.

i lean out the window

head crammed between two panes

as the rain starts to drum on the

ledge. brown paper bags float

in the gutter carried on a pothole

chimera and i titter: i told you

129

i was a pluviophile. all i wanted

were fourteen cream plumerias.

i claimed it a little in jest:

a prattle and a ramble rolled into

one ambiguous hairball. i avert

to the doorstep below where – lo

and behold! – there sat not thirteen

not fifteen but fourteen cream plumerias.

sodden and lovely and drenched.

privilege

i wake up with

female and *working class*

attached to me. but i

know that i am privileged

in having *white* attached

to me too. recognise

your privileges — we all

have them — and respect

boundaries. it is not a

joust or a horn-butting

competition but a case of

respect and acknowledgment.

its hard to live in the city

i your nymphet and you my suzerain

sit and strum guitar on verdant terrain

where foxgloves obscure our vision again

and our fingertips trace the ground in vain.

neither hand can produce an honest chord

and each note that falls flat is soon ignored

since i am your kitten and i you shall lord

over till i decide that i am bored

and hunt down another plaything or toy.

all the while one hand grips the corduroy

that cocoons my thigh as the other cloy

talon grasps at the wheel like a decoy.

we ride into the sun where red meets blue

and our lips crinkle in the moonlit dew,

my face spritzed with rosewater and yours too,

imparting gingham glances: is this true?

soul sisters of the seashore

we read our souls to one another

as clear as an ocean. recite the

scriptures like they are clockwork.

like they are sermon. this is the sea

that connects us, the waves and

ripples that nod into vicarious

elation and enriched experience.

you cackle until your sides start to

split at the seams and those eels

wobble at your shins. it is a gross

mud-pie convulsion that cakes your face

and drowns your entire body. submerged

in an ebb that is not too shallow

and not too deep. he is the sand

that trickles between your toes

and gets trapped inside your

dampened clothes. he makes you

happy and that makes me happy too.

nine ladies

nine ladies dine on oysters

in vienna where dreams

come to suppurate and

loiter on the tongue like

ethanol or nicotine. fatal

attraction and a nose tipped

with blush; it commands

attention so that the heart

might haunt the brain in

discourse and in temper.

figurine woman with gloss

slathered on her parted lips

and a cows lick that wrestles

with her milkmaid braid. i

watch you. you! one sock up

and one sock down. swathed

in a veil of tulle and chiffon.

a havisham with vogue spread

nude on the bed thats sheathed

in polka dot linen. we waltz

and our collarbones harmonise;

two xylophones that mould

the sweetest melodies known

to man.

memory lane

there are leaves in this

scrapbook; old rural

lanes and pastoral

autumns come to pass.

there is a smile and

a kiss from a mother

and a cousin, a potato

print and a bloodied

plaster from leaping over

ambitious turnstiles that

niggle at the kneecaps.

there are curvatures

and crevices and blots

littered with crisp packets

and sun-kissed spines.

papier-mâché people on

polystyrene cupholders.

this body has served me well

this body has served me well.

show me the wonder so that i might

marvel and muse upon the universe and

its sublime landscapes and the people

i have loved in the past. let me listen to

sweet music! gramophone records and

beaten up discs that rinse out all the

melancholia and solitude. i am not alone.

touch other mouths and touch the mouths their

lips have traced and their tongues have

brushed. tempt asseverations into

existence and spread tenderness.

move mountains. nurse me and invigorate

me. house me and shield me.
strengthen me

and coddle me. heal me and carry
me.

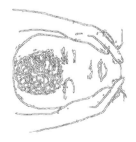

i must apologise.

a campsite

sundown. grasshoppers writhe in vegetation.
the firepit assails the white tents daubed in
muddied handprints. learned finger-puppets.
marshmallows shoved on skewers dangle over
dishonest flames that spit and sputter at the
sight. there goes a sheared sheep – a lamb
that is doomed to lie with a lion as the cow
leaps over the moon. it bleats over babys
breath rolled out for banquets and group
pictures. a backdrop. bruises under the skin
that have not appeared on top. pinafores and
portraits.

a very british childhood

i smoked candy sticks when i was eight years
old and the teachers rolled their eyes in scorn.
we jumped into dirtied puddles that would
pool into our wellington boots as the rain
hammered down on our heads where our
hoods had fallen prisoner to the wind. *man
down!* i dissected my saffron bun at lunch
and swapped fruit flakes with my friends
because i preferred them to dairylea dunkers.
we sat on wooden floors each morning
(promoted to benches when we reached ten
years old) and sang kumbayah − *give me oil
in my lamp keep it burning!* i hated p.e. so
tried to skive by claiming to have broken
my foot: "put a wet paper towel on it!"
the teacher would cry, "and you can wear
the shorts from lost property, too!" big red
things that could fit all your mates at once. it

wasnt so bad, being a kid. you dont know what you got till its gone.

pit-stop

oh! what a night, what a blast we would have

as we scrambled over the fields of glass

with checkerboard knees like a rubix cube

and whiskey tainting those broken-down

tongues.

we felt as though we were moving mountains

and that rules were made to be broken, right?

and that sentiment stays entirely true

except now we look back and still feel cool

cause we miss it, not because we live it

anymore. yes, its sad that you can be

blind to your privilege because school sucks

and you may not fit in or wear nice shoes

and you scoff at grown-ups who tell you that

these are the best years of your life! but

child, listen to me, it doesn't matter now -

the hierarchies, the netball game you missed
cause you pretended to sprain your ankle,
your physics homework you forged to stay out
of trouble, the words in the toilets and
the gum in your hair, you will look back

through your spectacles, rose-tinted they may
be, cause you always used to tell yourself
"will this all matter in five years, or one?"
hell no it doesnt! prophecy for the
ages, just dont disrespect what you had
and you lost cause time ran in circles and
you ended up stray and dizzy and drunk
because, my honey, it all seems stone-cold
sober now. dare you peep through time's
frosted looking-glass? cause nothing really
mattered in five years the first time, and it
won't again love. it didn't even matter in one.

he calls me by his name

black and white sit together

on the piano where the

bell-sleeved player wrings

his hands and cracks his

knuckles as he uses both

in conjunction. his composition

is palatable now. we exist

to love one another.

what makes a woman?

i am a strong woman

a bitch-i-can-do-anything-i-want woman

a prostitute and a whore

and a prude all rolled into one

fallible shell that the sun beats

down on and the rain smatters

square in the jaw. a veneer

lashed in mascara and concealer

to shield the world from the

colossal crescent moons beneath

each eye and the hormonal

pimples that wage war on my pores

which i lay bare whenever i want

to, wearing as little or as much

as i want to. i would rather die

than dry-shave so i dont care

which sad drip has to witness

these hirsute pits. i started my

period at a party last week and

everyone knew about it; i was

not embarrassed but simply

asked if anyone had a pad or a

tampon to spare. i will plunge

into a chignon of nachos dredged

in unspeakable amounts of sour cream

and guacamole or i will chug coffee

and munch on a salad with no dressing

because these choices shouldnt need

to be rationalised: i dictate the fuel:

i am the driver, you are the passenger.

football is a second home but supporters

with vaginas do not watch it just to

ogle the goalkeeper or the central

mid but should she do so then that is

neither-here-nor-there and should she

not watch it at all then that is also

neither-here-nor-there and does not

render her inferior or superior. the

biggest triumph? to dream up

whichever river or avenue a heart

might wish to persue in the assurance

that it will not remain a dream but

can, with determination and spirit,

become a reality; i can fight for

whatever position i want at

whichever corporation i wish

in whatever field i desire. we

are strong women: we like men,

we like women, we like no one,

we like everyone, we are black,

we are white, we are asian, we

are hispanic, we are faithful, we are

faithless, we want ten children,

we want no children, we are

underweight, we are overweight,

we are five feet tall, we are six

feet tall, we are everything in
between. we are strong women.

fainéant jazz

that piano climbs; it meanders up the
pavement and avoids each crack in the
slab. it darts across cast iron manhole
covers and coasts along chestnut benches.
the stroll – the jazz – greets me with
a gentle obeisance and drags me by the
hand to the next steaming cuppa joe and
buttery croissant. everything is okay.

view from a hot tin roof

irretrievable clouds disperse:

a distant hearth crackles in a

remote red-bricked cottage

with thatching on its rooftop

and oscillating ivy vines that

clamber and crawl through the

clefts.

we signpost the abandoned

warehouses and decrepit dumping

grounds from our vantage point —

omniscient. we taunt the glum

streetlamps as they droop their

heads and illuminate the drizzle.

we pleat into one.

its corrugated metal prods into

our denim synthesis as you leer

over me with one hand clenching

my bulbous trachea and plant

three kisses onto my forehead.

self-care

and that was when

i vowed to treat

myself far better

than you ever

treated me.

parenthood: a tale of evolution

when i was a little girl

you smooched each knee

that rasped on concrete

ground. raspberry coulis.

nursed each bruise. fixed

each splinter. plastered

up each graze. i climbed

trees with mum and played

dolls with dad. leaves pressed

on paper. lawnmower trimmings.

when i was a teenager

i cursed beneath the breath you

birthed. acidic tongue with barbs

for teeth: i was venomous. slammed

the doors you bloodied your hands

to upkeep. punched the walls you

hand-painted. rolled my churlish eyes.

defied in disobedience. ceased to

embark on our five-mile strolls

every saturday lunchtime.

when i was twenty-and-a-half

i realised that you did your best

to provide your best: clothes and

food and water and a room. we

didnt have much but we always

had enough and for that im truly

thankful. we watch the game together

and blare vinyl in the evenings. gossip

about any old sod who dares cross

our path. drink tea at breakfast and

cider at lunch — whiskey in rye

as a nightcap.

best-laid plans

one day i will scoop my children

into my arms, bundle them

up when the torrent

batters the pane

and the fire starts

to crackle, and tell

them that it will be

okay. because life is a

melting pot of experiences

(some euphoric, some

miserable, some coax

the heart, others smash

it into smithereens)

but i will remain at

your beck and call

for now and for ever.

we can make it

better in the end, child.

there is always a solution.

women supporting women

love one another: the other women

who walk home from work with

their keys wedged between their

middle and index fingers; the other

women who move to accomplish and

achieve so that their own daughters

may grow up in a kinder world; the

other women who dress up on a

saturday night and conduct the room

with an impish wave and a thigh-high

slit. *other* does not mean *marginalisation*

here but *in addition to*. we are tethered

in our experiences. our womanhood. their

gain is not your loss. and your loss is not

their gain.

treat yourself

i urge you to treat the symptoms

and nourish your soul

so that one day you might treat

the cause.

do you remember paris?

the rolling meadows were tangible in

the manner in which each bud did dot the

retina and pierce the iris with its

pox. the bulbs bore a jaundiced hue and the

light ensnared them in a mustard tincture.

to watch on them was to venerate them:

those hillside sirens coerced one into

voyeurism. it was exclusive yet

elusive; lorelei and ligeia

corporeal. each maiden weaved a word

as fine as golden thread that fluttered on

the mercurial zephyr and burrowed

into the porcelain heart that can bend

so shall never be broken (but is prone

to fissures and is fallible in its

flânerie). bookending the bloom were the

taraxacum which mottled the earth and

bruised the giggles with its ashen cinders.

they raped the forgotten nothings and the
unfinished goodbyes but sprout up from the
charcoal like painted quills in a stupor.
all is handsome convulsive and yellow.

moon-lady

let us send a woman to the moon so that

she should dance and weave amid the craters

in celebration. a colossal leap for womankind:

for the suffragettes; the underpaid; the

housewives; the career-women; the mutilated;

the child brides; the *'legally'* raped; the

illiterate and uneducated; the women we still

need to support and encourage

and aid as best we can. let us send a

woman to the moon so that she knows that

the sky is certainly not the limit. and that it

never will be again.

saccharine tears

faucet

like a faucet

the waterline seeps

a singed trachea –

or a sarcophagus

asphyxiate –

lets just pretend

it is honey

togetherness

we grow in tangent

a swan and a cygnet

in equal parts

decorum and respect

like a tulle-laden ballerina who

pirouettes across the pond

synchronised – having risen

and fallen – with each

petite droplet.

qu'est-ce que c'est

i look into the mirror and i see you,

little narcissus with shimmering eyes

of iridescent blue, piercing into the

chasm inside as though you

could swoop — medallion falcon

glazed in the golden - down

and squeeze the gasp

from my lungs, the esse from

my bones. chokehold! — my

chocolate waves curled with care

are not enough to seduce you

into giving up the fight, nor is

my tongue with its naysaying

nothings and prose and slapdash

rationale. i dont want to fight

you because i dont want to be

saved tonight. i am prey.

embrace ennui

hem your chelsea smile!

let us remove the yarn

and unthread each stitch

until it unravels into a tangled

thicket like cassette reel.

geranium strokes

i converse with malevolent

little whispers that titter

at the bottom of my teacup

where the leaves sit loose

like lacy doilies on a saucer

rimmed with pink petals and

traced in baby-haired lavenders.

crying is allowed

to cry is to heal — your

tears turn into ointment.

miscalculations

misshapen thank-yous

and mistaken identities –

santoku in the heart!

acquit this hideous

misinterpretation and

let me in. i need you.

time's inevitable passage

i pass bodies and minds littered

and liminal strewn around each

post-box and passage, each curb

and cost-cutter. i pass pasts:

dalliances and peccadillos

regrets (such an ugly word!)

aspirations and ambitions

insecurities peppered with

experience. i wish to learn

people.

do not loathe the lines or

anaemic strands that represent

time. it is no accident. we sail

on wooden rowboats and

paddle when the vessel

capsizes. slaves to the current.

head above the water. whims,

pipedreams or privilege; we are

all headed in the same direction

to the same plunge over the same

incandescent waterfall. and that

is salvation.

meet at the kitchen windowpane

and how will the rosebuds smothered in a

molten matter lose themselves and surrender

to the night and the noir paleness where

the hummingbird rests on his laurels

sanction his reticence with mathematics

and pragmatics? he perches on an olive

branch

and moans upon a wishing well: saccharine

is the aroma: french toast doused in brown

sugar.

what is love?

i like you in fragments

i hate you in morsels

yet each little segment

comes to form one

complete whole and we

call it love

the dandelion

the dandelion wavers in the heat,

shaking and reticent in her stature.

the dandelion is poignant and stiff,

but stronger than she could ever compute.

the dandelion thinks she is fruitful,

unfurling and offering her seeds

to unworthy and unnecessary

toxins and herbicides disguised as care.

173

the dandelion is feeding the ground,
fertilising that barren soil which formed
our void and tepid fleshly matter.
the dandelion is a hopeless cause,
romantic and wretched in her substance
undermined in her visceral being.

the dandelion spouts like a fountain.
defiant and difficult, vexatious
is she. she disperses and surges in
a climatic wave too feral to take.
it streams in fetters and forgeries and
apologies. i am sorry that she
is sorry. they fall back down and into
the ground where every fibre grew anew.
i loved her and i think that i love you.

christening the springtime

brilliant blue yonder! the skies part and i peer into off-white windowpanes where little old ladies perch in their recliners and slather their tea-cakes with butter as their lashes flirt with the sparrows. the pulp gathers at the bottom of their glasses, orange and mean. fresh grass trimmings wade into their airspace as the strapping neighbour mows with gusto and infiltrates their senses: transported to a universal space where the sun would shield over the helter-skelter rooftops – noble timekeeper – intent on staying put until the last bicycle wheel had ceased to spin and the final t-bar sandal had been wiped on the coarse doormat. prickles on naked soles. and the white houses would gleam like brass-necked pearls and the brown houses would bronze the impish breeze with a grin. sparse clouds wisped as the globe continued to roll – plump little felines. smooched the air. peppered the blue.

im sorry, darling

he stood, leant aloof against the doorframe

with a flannel shirt wrapped around his waist

and a juxtaposing ensemble of

a white t-shirt dappled with paint stains

and freshly pressed blue jeans that clung to

him. the day-before-yesterday's

stubble was dotted on his chin, smattered about

his lips. we woke up folded into one

another, interlaced in each other's

arms, bickering over trivial crap:

that his mother didn't invite mine to

their barbecue, that the pile of dishes

swimming about the sink was increasing

tenfold. we bathed in bleary-eyed silence

until he offered an impish eyebrow

raised to the heavens, and a coy cool smirk

that was stubborn, stupid, and jaded in

its nonchalance; lovably annoying,

an i-will-not-apologise-with-words

veneer. but he handed me a coffee

instead — black and instant with two sugars —

which i placed on the dresser because i

prefer my hot drinks lukewarm (much to his

bemusement). he watched as i brushed my

curls, and not a word penetrated the air,

since *'sorry'* — like *'love'* — can manifest in

more ways than one.

oh! to be sixteen

we ran through meadows with our hands

interlinked as the grass lashed at our

sunburnt calves and the dandelion seeds

bit at our dimples. a clement crescendo.

craftless

how curious that words do not

bend for a wordsmith when she

spots a man with the potential

to blot the wet cartridge and

gather up the pencil shavings.

people-pleaser

nothing is for everyone:

not the wisp on a willow

not the glimmer in a bayou.

it is impossible to sate

seven billion brains.

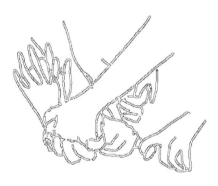

validate me

i am a woodpecker incarnate,

great and spotted and incubated

and validated, a metronome

murmur on the bonnet or the thatch.

fickle and faithless, notorious

creed, a baby pied piper drumming

on riverbank or sand-dune or home.

dearest friend

i volunteer to be a mirror

antique and golden dusted

carved in truths and legacies

to show you that not only are

you platinum on the outside

but an emerald within —

compassionate and intelligent

abrasive and assertive. a woman

far stronger than she could ever

imagine.

i once wanted to

drape bedsheets over every

mirror in the house and uncover

them five years later so that i

may look at myself objectively —

so that the rolls wouldnt matter

or the pimples or the nose with

a bump in it because i would

be an anonymous stranger. i want

to be your five-year-old mirror.

remove the sheets and marvel.

this is your home.

masters of the brush

i am proud to be part of a generation

that is allowing men to experiment with

mattes and shimmers; to conceal a ferocious

zit and have no shame in soothing his

combination skin with moisturiser. it is as

artistic as an impressionistic painting or contour

etching except he is the artist *and* the art

all at once: a simultaneous canvas and

a palette. that it has been gendered in the

past is wrong; we should all have the

credence to enhance and express ourselves as

we see apt with no time to mull over

anatomical and societal constraints.

that *feminine* becomes a pejorative is

wrong and it furnishes my heart to see that

we are growing ever-the-more accepting and

warm because when i was five i would have

pointed and laughed.

the accordion that played on its own

quelle folie! a locomotive streetscape with

cobbles that intertwine and tango into

tomorrow. transcend each cadaverous

gallop. the little ragamuffin dons

brogues and tosses pennies in his palm

as he scuds across the cobbles where

the insects hide out with the earlobes

and the painted eyelids hang agape

at the accordion that seems to play

on its own. it rests on a stool (and

cannot be moved) outside l'hôtel

du prince de galles where pigeons

cerebrate and guttersnipes sneer

at the timbre that echoes down

the twitchels like splenetic mirrors.

natural-born conqueror

limescale dots the cavern walls

so that i can polish it. ice invades

each antarctic crevice so that i

might wield this soviet icepick

and claw — tooth-and-nail —

to the summit. i have it within

me. i always had it within me no

matter who told me otherwise,

we are born mountaineers.

lost and found

i sat beneath a lemon
tree

and thought upon a
signet

coloured as a poppy

it floundered amidst a

rolling blue tide

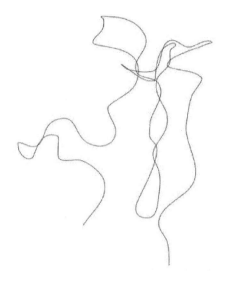

learning to forgive yourself

nourish the soul that brims with
potential. it is unique and deserves
all the treasures the world has to
share. adopt patience as your
lovechild and foster benevolence
so that karma shall wish to replenish
your fortunes with the energy you
choose to expel. but we are human:
we make mistakes and curse people
under our tongues and then curse
ourselves for our own callousness.
i invite you to extend an olive branch
and a warm palm to those that you
have upset or mistreated. that includes
you. you are too harsh on your spirit.
dress those wounds in bandages so that
you may allow yourself to bathe again
without the persistent sting of an ancient

incision and start afresh.

everything's coming up posies

seashell child! you have so much

to experience. push those daisies

into the soil and shovel them over!

cradled on bows that are liable to

collapse. but this is truth and kismet –

it happens to us all. nurse those

wounds. there will always be tomorrow.

so naïve little sparrow. honeysuckle bred.

nursed from the hive. why do you

lament? your adventure is nowhere near

complete; in fact it has scarcely begun.

a rallying call to survive

remember: you have endured moments that feel like a baseball bat to the kneecaps; days that feel like a farcical slog; people that have the power to sting the bees in return. you have endured the worst day of your life thus far and yet you are still here to read these words. and i hope that teaches you that you can overcome anything. i hope that reminds you that if you could get through that turmoil then you can sure as hell get through it a thousand times over and laugh in its face all the while cause you deserve to survive.

CONCLUSION

07/04/19:

I'm pleased that you're reading this and that you've made it to the end. It proves that you've done a far better job than I did; oftentimes, I don't care to read things back because I end up invalidating the content. Because when you emote with intense vigour, with black-and-white and all-or-nothing seeping through your veins, its an unusual experience to contemplate the retrospective scenario when everything is grey. It is easy to wonder why you felt a certain way about a certain situation or a certain person, it is easy to wonder why something that seems so insignificant now caused you so many sleepless nights, it is easy to wonder whether you were overreacting or whether you were being overdramatic. You weren't. You weren't because, in that moment, you *did* feel that way about a certain situation or a certain person, you *did* lose sleep over it, and it *did* invoke a strong emotional response. It's all about appreciating that you were hurt, or upset, or elated, or incensed. But you made it.

I'm pleased that you're reading this because it means that you made it, full stop. It means that you survived your worst day and, for whatever reason, decided to give me a chance along the road. We don't have to have anything in common or any shared experiences, but I hope that this collection (the truths, the mistruths, the soundbites, the reactions to given scenarios) have allowed you to muse upon your own circumstances – your own truths, your own supposed failures, your own highs, your own lows, and your own greys. I hope that you are able to appreciate that *your* existence is blotched with rye – sure! – but is, when all is said and done, bespattered with mulberries as well. It is a bittersweet filament. And it never goes out.

All the love,

SARAH MORRISH.

Below are my social media accounts. Follow me for more content (I do complain a lot but I am also hilarious, I promise!). But, most importantly, please do not hesitate to drop me a message with *anything* – questions, queries, dilemmas, anecdotes, rants – because I love connecting with new people and I love a good chinwag.

instagram: @sarahmorrishpoetry

twitter: @fioruccidove

blog: sarahmorrish98.wixsite.com/inklings

need copy written? check out my fiverr page: sarahmorrish98

business / collaboration enquiries: sarahmorrishpoetry@outlook.com

24732205R00111

Printed in Great Britain
by Amazon